AMAZING SPORTS STORIES FOR KIDS

Inspirational Athletes and Unforgettable Moments That Will Ignite Your Passion for Sports!

LEIGH JORDYN

© **Copyright 2023 - All rights reserved.**

The content contained within this book may not be reproduced, duplicated or transmitted without direct written permission from the author or the publisher.

Under no circumstances will any blame or legal responsibility be held against the publisher, or author, for any damages, reparation, or monetary loss due to the information contained within this book, either directly or indirectly.

Legal Notice:

This book is copyright protected. It is only for personal use. You cannot amend, distribute, sell, use, quote or paraphrase any part, or the content within this book, without the consent of the author or publisher.

Disclaimer Notice:

Please note the information contained within this document is for educational and entertainment purposes only. All effort has been executed to present accurate, up to date, reliable, complete information. No warranties of any kind are declared or implied. Readers acknowledge that the author is not engaged in the rendering of legal, financial, medical or professional advice. The content within this book has been derived from various sources. Please consult a licensed professional before attempting any techniques outlined in this book.

By reading this document, the reader agrees that under no circumstances is the author responsible for any losses, direct or indirect, that are incurred as a result of the use of the information contained within this document, including, but not limited to, errors, omissions, or inaccuracies.

INTRODUCTION

Hi! My name is Leigh Jordyn, a stay-at-home mom to three boys, and the inspiration for writing this book comes primarily from my boys' love of sports. The games themselves can, of course, be extremely entertaining and have us seated on the edge of our seats and chewing our fingers to the nub!

But it is important to remember that underneath all of the thunderous touchdowns, buzzer-beating three-pointers, and last-minute goals are athletes at the very top of their game.

Imagine how much early morning practice it took for Steph Curry to become a three-time NBA champion, how many hours a young Lionel Messi must have spent kicking his football against the wall, or all the traveling a young Tom Brady had to do for practice and football camps.

Their dedication is commendable and should be inspiring to all of us, which is why I decided to write this book, to not only inspire my own children but all of you guys and gals too!

The grit and determination that it takes for an athlete to make it as a professional, let alone to the top of their sport, as well as their refusal to give up on their dreams, is something that we can all learn from.

We will look at multiple athletes, both male and female, from a range of sports. Exploring their journeys, hardships, and triumphs so that hopefully, by the end, you will feel ready to reach for your own dreams, no matter how far-fetched they might feel. All of the athletes in this book started out feeling exactly the same way, and with hard work and perseverance—they not only made it but surpassed everyone's expectations!

So, let's dig in shall we, starting with the most popular sport in North America!

TABLE OF CONTENTS

Introduction iii

Chapter 1: American Football 1

    Tom Brady 2

    Michael Oher 6

    Jimmy Graham 9

    Jerry Rice 13

    Walter Payton 17

Chapter 2: Basketball 21

    Kareem Abdul-Jabbar 22

    Michael Jordan 26

    Steph Curry 30

    Giannis Antetokounmpo 35

    Terry Rozier 40

Chapter 3: Baseball 44

    Babe Ruth 45

    Jackie Robinson 50

    Jim Abbott 55

    Curtis Pride 60

    Pete Gray 65

Chapter 4: Soccer 70

    Lionel Messi 71

    Neymar 74

    Victor Moses 78

    Luka Modric 82

    Alireza Beiranvand 86

Chapter 5: Inspirational Women 91

    Jessica Long 92

    Bethany Hamilton 96

    Kathrine Switzer 100

    Serena Williams 105

    Lindsey Vonn 109

Conclusion 113

References 114

Chapter 1

AMERICAN FOOTBALL

American football is the most viewed sport in America, boasting viewing figures of 17.1 million in 2021 for their regular season! But that's not all; in 2023, it was estimated that over 113 million viewers tuned in to watch Super Bowl LVII making it the second highest-viewed game ever!

Its popularity and the revenue it drives are both huge, which means it's no surprise that its players provide some inspirational stories, but they aren't all rags-to-riches stories.

TOM BRADY

You guys know how many times I have been turned down in my life? To be told how many times that I couldn't accomplish something?
—**Tom Brady**

Before Tom Brady became arguably the biggest name in football, he was the ultimate underdog.

Don't believe me? Take a look at some of the notes from his NFL draft report back in 2000:

- Skinny and poor build
- Lacks strength and physical stature
- Lacks the ability to avoid the rush as well as mobility
- Lacks a really powerful arm
- Can't progress downfield with the ball
- Can't throw a really tight spiral
- A systematic player who can be exposed when forced to improvise
- Is knocked down too easily

Tom Brady lacked a *powerful arm*. Tom—Brady.

How did he overcome that? Sheer hard work. He outworked everybody. But before we get into that, let's hop back a little.

Tom was born in San Mateo, California, in 1977, the youngest of three siblings, all of which were sisters, which meant the little guy had it rough from the start! Far from the traditional sports prodigy, Tom didn't actually start playing until he was a freshman in high school. Most people that make it into the NFL have been playing since the 3rd grade!

Tom was a good yet unspectacular player; so unspectacular, in fact, that when he finally caught the eye of Michigan University, he found himself behind seven other quarterbacks on the depth chart—seven!

They were considered faster, stronger, and more athletic. The only way Tom was going to move them aside was through sheer hard work—and he outworked every single one of them. He had outshone six of them to take the backup spot by his sophomore year.

It took Tom another two whole years of working, improving, and refusing to quit to finally claim the starting spot at Michigan, but even the fact that he led his team to two bowl games wasn't enough for the NFL scouts.

Back in the year 2000, where after Tom's coach only received one call from the NFL, he took a chance in the draft which was nearly a disastrous move when he was the 199th pick; bear in mind there are only 250 picks in total!

With determination and heart, Tom stuck it out with the New England Patriots, desperate to show them, and all the NFL teams that had passed on him, that they were wrong.

He finally got his chance when the starting quarterback picked up an injury.

Twenty years, seven Super Bowls, and five MVPs later.

I think he proved his point.

What can we learn from Tom's journey from underdog to undeniable? Only *you* get to determine your potential.

Greatest Sporting Achievement

Tom Brady broke his *own record* by winning a seventh Super Bowl with Tampa Bay, beating defending champions Kansas City 31-9.

MICHAEL OHER

It's true that we can't help the circumstances we're born into and some of us start out in a much tougher place than other people. But just because we started there doesn't mean we have to end there.
—**Michael Oher**

Michael was one of 12 siblings, born in Memphis, Tennessee. Unfortunately, his start was as tough as it could be, with his mother suffering from addiction to both alcohol and drugs and his dad in and out of jail.

Unsurprisingly, this meant that Michael was lacking both a role model and any structure in his life. He struggled at school and had to repeat both first and second grade! In fact, things were so bad that he actually attended a total of 11 schools in his first nine years of education.

When he was just seven years old, he was put into foster care and bounced around multiple foster homes, along with sleeping on the street. Think about how easily Michael could have let his story be a sad one, but he didn't: He became a success.

Michael received his first much-needed *break* while sleeping on the couch of an athletic program director. He tagged along when the director took his son to a local Christian school, and eventually, seeing how tough life had been on Michael and wanting to give him a shot at redemption, the school gave Michael an opportunity too.

And when the opportunity knocked, Michael knocked it clean off its hinges. He got his head down, still staying on the sofas of friends and doing what he could to keep afloat, but putting his all into football and knowing that was his way to a better life.

It was around this time that he was presented with another major opportunity, meeting a wealthy Christian family who clothed him, fed him, and hired a tutor for him.

Eventually, his talent on the football field paid off in the form of an offer from the University of Mississippi, but not until he had worked hard to raise his grades, fighting just as hard in the classroom as he did on the football field.

Michael would excel at university, winning all-American honors that led to him being picked in the very first round of the NFL draft in 2009 by the Baltimore Ravens. He went on to win the Superbowl with the Ravens in 2013, completing his incredible redemption story.

There is plenty to learn from Michael's story, but the most important message is that no matter the start you are given, *you* decide your own ending.

Greatest Sporting Achievement

Michael Oher made the honor roll twice as a first-team All-American.

JIMMY GRAHAM

When I was a kid, I used to think about what my worth was.
—Jimmy Graham

Who defines one's *worth?*

Before Jimmy Graham had a net worth of $12 million, he was born in North Carolina, and his upbringing was about as tough as it gets. Having multi-racial parents and thus being mixed race, he was often treated as an outcast that struggled to fit in.

When he was just 9 years old, a disagreement over $98 led to his stepdad, the man closest to Jimmy, dropping him off at Social Services. After a short period with his mom and her horrible boyfriend, just two years later, his mom dropped him off at a group home where he was bullied by the bigger, older children.

Jimmy's mom dropped him off because she struggled to pay the bills, but after just nine months, she brought him back home to stop the bullying. For Jimmy, things would only get worse in the form of an even bigger bully—his mom's new boyfriend.

Jimmy was made to feel like he wasn't worth the money or time needed to raise him. In fact, it was only when he met a counselor at a weekly prayer group that the bullying stopped, and he was in an environment where he could not only heal but also grow. He was finally told that he was smart and shown that someone could see the value in him.

Despite his fame later coming from football, it was actually Jimmy's basketball talent that was his saving grace. When he was in high school, a church youth counselor adopted him and helped him not only improve his grades but also gave him the chance to show his basketball talent as a sophomore while at a Christian Community College. His talent eventually saw him earn a basketball scholarship at the University of Miami.

It was the love and self-worth that Jimmy finally gained that encouraged him to grow, getting straight A's and, eventually, his scholarship.

As Jimmy grew older, so did his positive message. He wasn't bitter and didn't hold grudges; instead, he saw his suffering as an important part of his success—we can all heal, no matter who is reading this or what you are going through, pain is never permanent, and scars heal if you let them.

Now, Jimmy shares his story to inspire kids just like you, determined to show that only you can decide what your value is and that there's no limit to what you can achieve.

Jimmy Graham, the kid once *not worth* $98 dollars a month, now has a net worth of, again, $12 million—12—how? By refusing to let someone else determine what his value was.

So, who defines one's worth? Who defines your worth?

One person...

You.

Greatest Sporting Achievement

Jimmy Graham is ranked second in the all-time rankings for most receiving yards and receiving touchdowns by a tight end in a season.

JERRY RICE

*Today I will do what others won't, so tomorrow I will do what
others can't.* —**Jerry Rice**

Jerry Rice is widely regarded as the best receiver in NFL history. Some may even argue he's the best player, regardless of position.

Jerry was one of eight siblings, born in Crawford, Mississippi. His dad was a bricklayer, so he and his brothers would help him build houses over the summer, meaning that from a young age, Jerry was out working hard!

He played football from a young age but wasn't able to earn himself a scholarship. It was Mississippi State Valley University that gave him a chance. He grabbed it, fueled by the need to prove himself without a scholarship. Jerry and his teammates' passing attack actually received national attention—Jerry managed to catch 112 receptions and 1,845 yards with 27 touchdowns! This, along with finishing 9th in the Heisman voting and being named an All-American, was crazy for a kid from a small school!

But how did he do it? He never stopped working.

Unlike many in this book that tell tales of being obsessed with their chosen sport, Jerry was obsessed with hard work. His workouts are now the stuff of legend. He would do two hours of cardio, usually running up a huge hill, six days a week, and *then* three hours of strength training in the afternoons.

If you want an idea of just how tough that is, go and run up your nearest hill a couple of times and feel the burn in your thighs! He was doing that six days a week, without fail, *with* strength training!

Jerry knew that he wasn't the strongest or especially fast, but that didn't mean he couldn't work the hardest. He was driven by the same thing that a lot of us fear, but Jerry wasn't scared of failing or losing; he was scared he would disappoint his father.

But I can see you scratching your head. He wasn't especially fast? He was a wide receiver! This is the most amazing part of Jerry's story and the biggest lesson we can take from it. He worked hard, harder than everybody, but he also knew *what* to work hard on.

Rather than focus blindly on speed, he knew what areas he would need to be good in to be a good wide receiver.

He learned precise run patterns to dodge defenders, meaning he didn't need to be the fastest. His six days a week of weight training meant he was very strong, and his trail running meant he could change direction quickly and unpredictably. All that uphill running gave him incredible acceleration as well as building the stamina that helped him outlast opponents. While most were losing puff in the fourth quarter, Jerry was often fresh as a daisy!

Now, the hard work paid off for Jerry, and he's in not one but four Halls of Fame!

Jerry is a great example of outworking everyone in the right places. You don't have to be the best at everything, just at the things that matter to you, because the only person you are really competing with is yourself. We can also learn from the benefit of having a routine. Jerry was consistent and stuck to his plan even on the days that were harder to get out of bed.

Work as hard as you possibly can. And *even* smarter than that.

Greatest Sporting Achievement

Jerry Rice is sitting at the very top of the all-time receiving yards list with 22,895.

WALTER PAYTON

If you forget your roots, you've lost sight of everything.
—**Walter Payton**

American football is a tough sport. The heavy hits, bone-crunching snaps, cracks of heavy helmets colliding, big burly players under their shoulder pads, snarling, ready to go to war for their teammates. This is why a player nicknamed "Sweetness" stands out a little bit.

When Walter's father died young, he could have stumbled down the wrong path, as so many do without a strong father figure. Instead, he kept his head down and focused on his love of music before eventually turning to football.

He's now known as one of the most influential football players of his time. Despite celebrating incredible success, he is equally admired for his soft-spoken and humble demeanor.

But Walter nearly never even played football, not wanting to compete with or take the spotlight from his older brother. Out of loyalty, he initially refused to join the team, only agreeing after his brother's graduation.

If the above was a testament to Walter's character, his ability to pick the game up so quickly was surely a testament to his natural talent. His first high school carry resulted in him running sixty-five yards for a touchdown!

Walter's loyalty would show itself once more when he boycotted spring practices in protest of his head coach being demoted to assistant. Walter would, of course, return, eventually drafted in the first round of the 1975 draft by the Chicago Bears.

Yet, neither his fame nor his wealth ever steered him from his values, so much so that he was well-known for refusing to trash talk, giving credit to his teammates, and would go on to donate millions of dollars to charity.

But that's not all...

Unlike some of the sports stars in this book, who we have explored the birth and upbringing of, Walter Payton's loudest message was told at the end of his life. Unfortunately, he was diagnosed with a rare liver disease that needed a transplant to prevent death.

Staring certain death in the face, Walter could have used his celebrity status to move himself up the list of over twelve thousand awaiting a liver transplant. But he didn't, refusing to see himself as above anyone, he ultimately died in the same humble manner that he lived his life.

What can we learn from Walter? Humility, hard work, selflessness. That we are all equal; no amount of success could or should change that.

Greatest Sporting Achievement

Walter Payton had the *NFL Man of the Year Award* renamed to the *Walter Payton Man of the Year Award* to honor his legacy.

Chapter 2

BASKETBALL

American football might be the most popular sport in the US, but basketball is widely considered the most played, which isn't a surprise given how easy it is to grab a ball and throw it at a hoop in comparison to the equipment needed for football! Basketball is also considered popular worldwide, inside the top 10 when it comes to popularity.

KAREEM ABDUL-JABBAR

> *I would suggest that teachers show their students concrete examples of the negative effects of the actions that gangsta rappers glorify.*
> **—Kareem Abdul-Jabbar**

Even though he played basketball, Kareem Abdul-Jabbar was much, much more than just a basketball player. He used his status to benefit society and to be a role model for children that were in danger of losing their way.

Kareem was actually born Ferdinand Lewis Alcindor Jr. He was the only child of a department store worker and a transit police officer-slash-jazz musician. He was *always* tall for his age. In fact, he was already five feet eight inches by the time he turned nine.

Ironically, as a teenager, Kareem hated the height that would become such a huge asset in his career due to being stared at and being talked about—now, people stare at him for a very different reason! By the time he was 14, he was over six and a half feet tall *and* could dunk a basketball.

His NBA career was unmatched and unparalleled. He set records for points, blocks, and most career games. He even ranks as number two in the ranking for players with the most total points, only behind LeBron James. At the time of hanging up his jersey, he had collected a huge variety of accolades, including being a six-time NBA champion, and six-time NBA MVP, and he was even inducted into the Naismith Memorial Basketball Hall of Fame in 1995.

But as I said, he was much, much more than that.

Kareem was a social justice warrior who used his significant platform to fight for the little guys. Fighting to change public policy and opinion so that we live in a more balanced world. These are much more common now (think Colin Kaepernick), but it was less so back then.

He started his work, which would span sixty years, at a very young age, and rubbed shoulders with the likes of Muhammad Ali, John Carlos, and Billie Jean King.

His most prominent work came in the form of his fight against racism and racial inequality. He used his considerable height to stand against any form of inequality or discrimination, standing for the rights of the Native Americans, women, and the LGBTQ community. He also stood against anti-Semitism and all forms of religious intolerance.

His work hasn't gone unnoticed. He was honored with the *Friends of Simon Wiesenthal Center's Spirit of Hope Award* for his work building bridges between communities and contributions to human rights and social justice causes.

In the present day, Kareem is the longest-standing social justice athlete-activist, still fighting for the underrepresented to this day. His work outside of the court transcended his work on it. How many players that invented their own signature move can say that? Google the sky hook!

What can be learned from Kareem's journey? *A lot.* But let's focus on what he focused on, treating others equally regardless of race, gender, or beliefs.

Greatest Sporting Achievement

Kareem Abdul-Jabbar had the most career games in the NBA (at the time of retirement).

MICHAEL JORDAN

I've missed more than 9,000 shots in my career. I've lost almost 300 games. Twenty-six times, I've been trusted to take the game winning shot and missed. I've failed over and over and over again in my life. And that is why I succeed.
—**Michael Jordan**

Failure is an illusion.

As a player, Michael Jordan is remembered as one of the greatest, but the road to greatness is never easy, and even the great MJ was no exception to this. Michael's story is not only one of hard work but, most importantly, learning from defeat, never staying down after taking a hit, and getting back up even stronger.

When he was young, he was blessed with working-class parents that taught him the value of hard work as well as life skills. He was kept as far from street life as possible, and his mom taught him how to clean, do laundry, and even sew.

Michael was always fiercely competitive and was always reaching for things outside of his skill level, believing his heart would fill in the gaps. When he was a sophomore in high school, he tried and failed to make the varsity team because of his lack of height.

With that in mind, do we really think that it's a coincidence that he's now famed for his trademark spring? If he didn't have the natural height, he would jump higher. If you're not familiar with the term *Air Jordan*—go look it up!

He ran home, locked himself in his room, and sobbed, embarrassed and hurt—but it was that rejection that lit a fire under Michael, fueling daily practice sessions that would see him dragged from the gym at the start of the first period.

> *Whenever I was working out and got tired and figured I ought to stop, I'd close my eyes and see that list in the locker room without my name on it, that usually got me going again.*

Undeterred by his failure, he knew he had to get better. He swallowed his pride and earned a spot on the junior varsity team. But Michael found himself on the bench handing out towels and water to his teammates, so he got frustrated again.

So he knuckled down, upping practice and refusing to accept his spot on the bench. His work ethic, refusal to accept a spot on the bench, and a timely growth spurt gave him the springboard to become the team's star player, averaging more than 20 points a game.

He was then selected for the NCAA All-American First Team in both his sophomore (1983) and junior (1984) seasons. If he had let the first rejection put him off, Michael Jordan, the NBA legend, would never have existed.

A legend that would go on to win: NBA Rookie of the Year, five NBA MVP crowns, and six NBA championships, and would unsurprisingly see him inducted into the Hall of Fame. Now imagine if he'd locked himself in his room, cried all night, and woken up without ever playing basketball again!

Off the court, Michael has donated hundreds of millions of dollars to charity. Most notable is his incredible work as the Chief Wish Ambassador for the *Make-A-Wish Foundation*, an organization dedicated to granting the wishes of critically ill children. He has granted over 200 wishes and donated and raised a combined total of more than $15 million to the charity.

Michael Jordan is an icon, but he wasn't born one. His losses, setbacks, and missed shots helped mold him into one. He never gave up. You will all face rejection and be told *no*. It's what you do with that rejection that will define your future success.

Greatest Sporting Achievement

Michael Jordan won not one, but two three-peats with the Chicago Bulls.

STEPH CURRY

When it comes to basketball, I was always the smallest kid on my team. I had a terrible, ugly, catapult shot from the time I was 14 because I wasn't strong enough to shoot over my head, and I had to reconstruct that over the summer and it was the worst three months of my life. You'd think there are no hurdles or obstacles that I had to overcome, but even when I got to high school, I wasn't ranked. I wasn't ranked. I wasn't highly touted as a high school prospect. I had nobody really running, knocking on my door saying 'Please, please, please come play for our school. **—Steph Curry**

In a world so often filled with stress, challenges, and hardship, it's no surprise that Steph's joyous nature captured the attention and hearts of so many. He was the ultimate example of David slaying Goliath if David was always smiling and dancing.

But before we talk about who Steph became, let's start with who he started as.

Steph was born in Akron, Ohio, but he grew up in North Carolina, where his father played for the Charlotte Hornets, an NBA team. I know, I know, his dad was an NBA player; it's in his blood. What's inspirational about that?! Give me time, and we'll get there, I promise.

Steph's love for the game existed early. As a child, he would shoot during the Hornet's warm-ups with his brother, and the pair would even play on the court after hours. His love of basketball is no surprise, nor is his desire to follow in his father's footsteps.

Despite learning the game from his father and being immersed in the game from a young age, as a high school sophomore, Steph was only five feet six and weighed one hundred and twenty-five pounds, which was considered far too small to play pro ball. He was even forced to shoot from his waist due to his lack of strength!

Steph worked all summer with his father to get him shooting correctly, pushing his arms so far, he would often be left in tears. It paid off in a technical sense and fixed his shooting technique, but it wasn't enough, and he didn't receive any scholarship offers. Thus, we have our David!

In fact, the only major college that *did* extend Steph an offer was Virginia Tech, his father's alma mater. But even they only wanted him as a *walk-on,* meaning he would have to pave his own way, showing a distinct lack of belief in him.

Steph stayed patient, believing that the right coach and school would come along, and it did, in the form of Davidson College in North Carolina, a less favorable college with a lesser basketball program, not that it was enough to stop him.

In Steph's sophomore season, he had grown to six foot three, still not particularly tall in the world of basketball, and in his freshman year, he averaged twenty-one and a half points per game, the most in the country of all first-year players.

He had the attention of the nation, leading the 10th-seeded Davidson Wildcats to the Elite Eight of the NCAA (National Collegiate Athletic Association) with his signature three-pointer, as accurate and deadly as David's slingshot.

In his Junior season, Steph's average of twenty-eight point six points per game was the best in the country, and he was named a first-team All-American. The following is an excerpt from NBA Draft.net, analyzing Steph's weaknesses before the 2009 NBA draft: *"Far below NBA standard in regard to explosiveness and athleticism. At 6-2, he's extremely small for the NBA shooting guard position."*

Steph would go on to be selected by the Warriors in the first round of the 2009 draft and was voted as the runner-up for the Rookie of the Year. He simply *refused* to let his lack of size hold him back.

I would love to tell you that's where his struggles ended, but he had one more beast to confront in the form of ankle ligament damage that required six months of grueling rehabilitation and a combination of mental and physical strength.

How did Steph deal with the setback? By winning 4 NBA titles and being named the MVP twice, including making history as the league's first unanimously voted MVP in history.

Too small, huh?

Kids, it's *never* about the size of the dog in the fight and *always* about the size of the fight in the dog.

Greatest Sporting Achievement

Steph Curry won the NBA MVP in 2015.

GIANNIS ANTETOKOUNMPO

Before I leave this earth, I'm going to help people have a better future.

—Giannis Antetokounmpo

A lot of the athletes in this book grew up with very little, but Giannis grew up with even less, born into a foreign country without an identity.

Giannis was born in Sepolia, a working-class neighborhood and migrant area in Athens, Greece. His parents, both migrants from Nigeria, had originally intended to go to Germany so that his father could play semi-professional soccer out there—but a career-ending injury put a stop to that!

So, his parents land in Sepolia, and things are tough, real tough. Both struggled to find work due to being undocumented, and because Greece didn't offer birthright citizenship, it was going to be just as hard for Giannis and his brothers, who weren't considered Greek.

Giannis and his family would sell things in the street to make whatever money they could and would go hungry most days. Giannis considered himself the best salesman. His secret? Persistence. *"My secret was that I would never give up. I would continue asking people until I could get them to buy something. It also helped that I was young and sweet."*

He shared a bed with his brothers and lived in constant fear of eviction as they struggled to pay rent, dealing with stresses far beyond his years. Young Giannis had no idea how well that mental toughness would serve him in the future.

So how did Giannis manage to get from selling things on the street to playing in the NBA? Thanks, in part, to a big slice of good fortune *or* a higher power of sorts, but I'll let you all decide that for yourselves.

While playing tag in the street with his brothers, the then 13-year-old Giannis was spotted by a native who had a feeling, an intuition, a message from God. Whatever it was, it changed the lives of Giannis and his family.

Impressed by Giannis' athleticism, he took him and his brothers to a local basketball team in the Greek suburbs. Giannis was never really interested in basketball, preferring to follow in his father's footsteps as a soccer player. It was his coach that convinced him that playing basketball may provide his family some much-needed money (boy, was he right!), and once Giannis and his brothers *did* start playing basketball, they actually had to share a pair of sneakers, preventing them from playing at the same time!

Giannis was noticed for the first time in his life, but the road to the NBA from a Greek A2 team was still going to be a near-impossible one. Thanks to his brother Thanasis's agent, grainy videos of Giannis playing were sent to International NBA scouts. Thanasis now plays in the NBA!

The videos were awful in quality and didn't show the scouts much due to the poor quality of the opposition, but two things were undeniable—Giannis had the athleticism and court vision. Thirty NBA scouts and general managers flew out to see him play, but only two had any concrete interest—Milwaukee and Atlanta.

Milwaukee took a punt, drafting a kid that didn't even know how to lift weights but had bundles of charisma. Once Giannis did get on the court, he was lucky enough to get the chance to show his skills when a few players on the team got injured. He was in the spotlight and had more money than he had ever imagined, but he never changed.

Saving most of the money that he did have for when his family was able to join him, Giannis *never* forgot where he came from. He was so uncomfortable with his newfound wealth that he once refused to sleep on the bed of the fancy hotel room that the team provided and slept on the floor instead!

Time passed, and Giannis provided all that he wanted, and more, for his family. On the court, he grew in stardom, winning his first NBA championship in 2021 and two MVP awards.

But off the court, both he and his brother remained incredibly grounded and humble. They established the *AntetokounBros Academy,* a charity founded to help provide children from Greece and Africa with opportunities that they weren't afforded growing up.

Giannis' story is one of faith, hope, and humility.

Greatest Sporting Achievement

Winning consecutive NBA MVP awards in 2019 and 2020, Giannis Antetokounmpo is one of only three players to win two before he was twenty-six—alongside Kareem Abdul-Jabbar and LeBron James.

TERRY ROZIER

I wake up every day like, 'How can I get better, how can I help my teammates be successful? I try to control what I can control and worry about us, nothing else. **—Terry Rozier**

Terry had a very dysfunctional childhood, so dysfunctional in fact that the odds of him still being around, let alone starring in the NBA, were very slim.

Born in Youngstown, Ohio, Terry was an energetic and enthusiastic child, throwing socks into milk cartons as a form of a makeshift basketball game. He always lacked a consistent father figure due to his dad being in and out of prison for a variety of offenses.

Unfortunately, when Terry was just six years old, he felt the consequence of his father's actions when he had to be taken from his mother. Criminal enemies of his father had threatened Terry, and his mother wasn't taking any chances with her baby boy.

He moved in with his grandmother, where he would sleep with a bag filled with his belongings, longing for his mother—he wanted to go home. He hated his grandmother because he blamed her for taking him from home, far too young to understand the dangers of returning home.

He would scream, cry, and lash out at his grandmother, forcing her to pin him to the floor until he calmed down. When others would have sent Terry to a foster home or juvenile detention center, his grandmother refused, telling him; *"I don't care how much you dislike me, I love you and you cannot do nothing to make me send you back to Youngstown, you're gonna realize, one day, how much I love you."*

That day would come years later when someone threatened his grandmother's house. She took Terry and his siblings into a back room and cried, fearing an attack, poised to escape out of a back window.

Thankfully nothing happened, but something changed in Terry that day. He saw, truly, how much his grandmother loved him and was sure to tell her. Emphasizing the point when he was 14 and had both his mom's and grandmother's names tattooed to his forearms, as well as his father's face and the word *"motivation"* as a constant reminder of the life he was rising above.

After his father had a brief stint of freedom, he was sent back to prison again, and this time, Terry found focus, moving back in with his grandmother willingly and putting everything he could into making his basketball dreams a reality.

He spent the majority of his time in middle and high school in the gym, working on his basketball skills and starring for his high school varsity team in his freshman year. But all of that came at a cost, with his grades suffering.

Meaning when Louisville came calling, his dream school, no less, he couldn't enroll. Undeterred, Terry spent a year at the Hargrave Military Academy, where he improved his grades and improved as a person, *"Hargrave made me mature, it made me grow up, and I needed that."*

Once Terry *did* get to Louisville, he never looked back.

With the number "3" emblazoned on his journey to symbolize his fresh start, he became one of the top prospects for the 2015 draft and eventually was picked by the Boston Celtics as the 16th overall pick.

Terry is still actively playing, and his career has seen him provide a better life for not only the family that got him through such a tough childhood but now for his own son, too, as he seeks to break the cycle that he was born into.

Greatest Sporting Achievement

Terry Rozier was selected in the first round of the 2015 NBA draft by the Boston Celtics.

Chapter 3

BASEBALL

The sport that is considered America's national pastime. Baseball has been a mainstay in US culture for over one hundred and fifty years, and its players have some of the most inspirational stories of all, as well as being some of the biggest stars in world sport, starting with an absolute legend...

BABE RUTH

You just can't beat the person who never gives up. —**Babe Ruth**

Babe Ruth. It doesn't matter whether you like baseball or even sports at all—everyone has heard the name at least once. An American baseball star turned cultural icon, Babe is renowned by many as the greatest player to ever play the game.

He set multiple records on his way to becoming a symbol of what it meant to be an American, skyrocketing baseball's popularity with his base-clearing home runs and leaving an everlasting legacy.

But before he was *Babe,* he was George Herman Ruth Jr.

Born in Baltimore, Maryland, Babe had a fight on his hands from the very beginning and was one of only two of his parents' eight children to survive infancy. They lived in a poor neighborhood, and his father worked his way through job after job to support them.

His father's absence meant that Babe was neglected. Slipping through the cracks, Babe would skip school, drink alcohol, and fight with others. His parents eventually had enough and shipped him off to an orphanage when he was just seven years old. Babe was a delinquent, and they couldn't handle him.

Babe spent most of the next 12 years at the orphanage, where he would be blessed with an education, as well as learning various skills. He worked as both a shirtmaker and a carpenter at a young age which actually allowed him to adjust his own shirt collars later on in his career!

It was the orphanage's sporting director that actually encouraged Babe to give baseball a try. He started as a catcher despite left-handers rarely playing in that position and had to wear a right-handed glove because of it.

It wasn't long before Babe became the best pitcher at the orphanage, and when he was 18, he was given permission to leave campus for weekend games. The director that encouraged him, Brother Herman, is someone that Babe had massive respect for and would praise for the rest of his life.

Babe's life would be changed forever in 1914 when he signed his first professional baseball contract. This was also when he would be given the nickname "Babe," as his old teammates joked that he was their coach's baby due to his treatment of him!

Babe joined the legendary Boston Red Sox and excelled. Just five years later, in fact, he would set the record for the most home runs in a season. It was off of the back of that success that he joined the New York Yankees, where he would go on to spend most of his career. He was paid $100,000, the highest amount that had ever been paid for a baseball player at that time.

His 15-season stint at the Yankees put him on the map, playing over 2,000 games, breaking batting records left, right, and center, *and* eventually ending his career with a jaw-dropping 714 runs—a record that would stand for 28 years!

Babe was notorious for refusing to rest on his laurels and pushing to be the very best. His work ethic and rise from an orphanage to an icon isn't the only reason he is an inspiration to so many.

He played at the time of the great depression when people *needed* hope. His incredible story helped people believe that anything was possible. Babe would even visit sick fans in hospitals. He would return to his hometown of Maryland to help children improve their baseball skills and was always happy to pose for pictures and sign autographs, staying in tune with the unruly child that he once was. *"I won't be happy until we have every boy in America between the ages of six and sixteen wearing a glove and swinging a bat."*

Babe's contribution and impact were so great. In fact, in 2018, Babe was posthumously awarded the Presidential Medal of Freedom.

Greatest Sporting Achievement

Babe Ruth has hit 40 home runs per season for 11 seasons—a record yet to be beaten!

JACKIE ROBINSON

A life is not important except in the impact it has on other lives.
—Jackie Robinson

Jackie Robinson was the MLB's first African-American player, crossing and ultimately removing the *color barrier* that existed at the time. Before Jackie took to the first base for the Brooklyn Dodgers, players of color were only allowed to play in the *negro leagues*.

As you can imagine, Jackie was subjected to abuse from the stands rife with racism, higher-ups in the game rejected his participation, and even opposition players did their best to injure him. He rose above all of it to not only survive but thrive, winning the *Rookie of the Year Award* that would later be named after him to honor his legacy. He was the first African-American player inducted into the National Baseball Hall of Fame.

On the 50th anniversary of his breaking the color barrier, his number was permanently retired from the game. April 15th has been dubbed *Jackie Robinson Day* by the MLB.

Unbelievable, right? But before all that.

Jackie was born in Cairo, Georgia, the youngest of five. When his father abandoned the family, his mother moved them to Pasadena, California, where she worked multiple jobs to support them. Pasadena wasn't a bad place to live, but Jackie's family was poor, and along with the small black community they were part of, they found themselves cut off from the rest of the locals.

It was Jackie's sporting prowess that would start to change his family's fortunes, and he was incredibly gifted. He earned varsity letters in baseball, basketball, football, and track from John Muir High School.

He continued to excel in all four sports at Pasadena Junior College, and when his older brother died, he decided to enroll at UCLA in his memory. He definitely made him proud by becoming the first student from John Bruin high school to earn four varsity letters in baseball, basketball, football, and track. He even won the NCAA long jump championship. Jackie Robinson was *very* gifted.

In some of the stories we have read, this is the point where professional teams would swarm Jackie for his services. But the world was a different place then. Jackie needed to support his mom, leaving college early and accepting a role as an athletics administrator.

However, his love of sports refused to die. He played semi-professional football for integrated teams (teams without racial division) in Hawaii and California until fate would play a role.

In 1942, Jackie was drafted into the US Army during World War II. Although Jackie never saw combat, he had a very different fight on his hands.

When he boarded a bus in Texas and refused to sit at the back, as were the rules at the time to keep those of color separate from the others, he was threatened with punishment from the US government. He was eventually let off. This was an example of his willingness to fight for equality without fear of the consequences.

Jackie left the army, and, needing somewhere to land, took a job as a basketball coach in Texas, completely unaware that he was heading for the most important chapter of his life.

Just one year later, Jackie was signed by Kansas City Monarchs, a team in the *negro league,* and starred in his very first season. The universe had a plan for Jackie, and fate would have it that scouts were watching the *negro leagues* at the time to find the players that not only had the physical strength for the MLB but the mental strength to endure the abuse and pressure that would come with being a poster boy for integration.

Jackie was one of many picked out and interviewed. When discussing the inevitable racial abuse that he would be faced with, Brooklyn Dodgers executive Branch Rickey told Jackie that he was looking for someone "with guts enough not to fight back."

Jackie went on to have a stellar career, broke down barriers, led the MLB's integration, and was an inspiration to all. He was named on *Time's* list of *the 100 most influential people of the 20th century* in 1999.

Greatest Sporting Achievement

Jackie Robinson led the Dodgers to six World Series and one Championship in ten years.

JIM ABBOTT

There are millions of people out there ignoring disabilities and accomplishing incredible feats. I learned you can learn to do things differently, but do them just as well. I've learned that it's not the disability that defines you, it's how you deal with the challenges the disability presents you with. And I've learned that we have an obligation to the abilities we DO have, not the disability.
—Jim Abbott

Jim Abbott was a professional baseball pitcher like no other. Born without his right hand, he adapted and refused to let the disability he was born with hold him back, proving that no amount of adversity should hold one back from their dreams.

Jim was born in Flint, Michigan. He was raised by his father, a sales manager, and his mother, who was a lawyer. After they tried to teach Jim how to use a prosthetic device, it became clear that he wasn't comfortable, and the decision was made for Jim to learn to live independently, living *with* his disability as opposed to trying to work around it—and boy, did he live!

Because of Jim's love for sports, his parents suggested soccer to get around his disability, but once again, Jim didn't want to *get around* anything, and he *loved* baseball. It was around this time that Jim's father helped him develop the technique that would help him make it to the very top—the Abbott switch—Jim would wear a glove on the end of his wrist arm while pitching, then switch the glove to his left hand when fielding.

But it wasn't easy and required countless hours of pitching against a brick wall and switching the glove back and forth for Jim to perfect it. But perfect it he did because he wasn't taking no for an answer. He would dream of being a professional ballplayer and imagine he was his favorite pitcher, Nolan Ryan.

Even when Jim entered *Little League,* he outshone his opponents. When he was just 11 years old, he threw a no-hitter that ended after five innings thanks to the mercy rule (essentially, he was beating them so badly the game ended out of mercy for the losing team). He was gaining attention from both admirers and detractors, with opposing coaches trying to find a way to take advantage of his supposed handicap. They couldn't.

In high school, he was even the lead quarterback for the football team leading them to the finals of the Michigan State Championship. Despite having clear football prowess too, his heart was in baseball, and he was off to the University of Michigan on a baseball scholarship.

Jim enrolled at the University of Michigan as the respected athlete that he had been striving to become.

His stature only grew once there, leading the Wolverines to a six, and two freshman records that saw them win the *Big*

Ten Title. He would continue to impress, winning the *Golden Spike Award,* an annual award presented to an outstanding college baseball player in the US. He eventually left the school with an impressive career record of 26 wins and eight defeats.

His next big milestone came in the form of carrying the flag for Team USA at the *Pan-American Games,* where the US defeated Cuba, on Cuban soil, for the first time in 25 years, before winning the gold medal at the summer games for his country, the following year!

Jim's Olympic heroics led to him joining the California Angels and making his professional debut during spring training, making it to the Major League without playing a single game in the minors!

Although Jim was adapting to, and thriving with, his disability. He never wanted to be known for it, which meant that when he eventually made his professional debut, and it was seen by many as a publicity stunt—it stung. *"I wanted the attention that comes from being successful, but I was very reluctant to draw any attention to my disability."*

More determined to prove his worth as a player, and despite struggling early on in his rookie season, Jim showed the mental strength to prove everybody wrong and win twelve games with a 3.92 ERA. Better yet, those twelve wins were more than any other rookie without Major League experience had managed previously, putting him in the record books.

Jim went on to have a stellar career in the MLB, known as a great player and not the novelty act that he feared he might be seen as. Today Jim actually works as a motivational speaker, supporting and inspiring others. How cool is that?

Greatest Sporting Achievement

Jim Abbot's most famous high point is perhaps throwing a no-hitter for the New York Yankees at Yankee Stadium in 1993.

CURTIS PRIDE

I felt it helped me a lot, it (his disability) allowed me to focus on the task at hand and not let the noise bother me. It has given me like a sixth sense and to be able to anticipate better.
—Curtis Pride

Another athlete that simply refused to let his disability stand in the way of his dreams, Curtis Pride is a former outfielder who was born deaf. A triple threat, Curtis excelled in baseball, basketball, and soccer, an immensely talented athlete. He saw his disability as a superpower, a sixth sense, allowing him to slow things down and block out the distracting noise around him.

Deafness didn't run in Curtis' family, so when he was born deaf, it was a surprise and was said to be caused by his mother having measles while pregnant. He worked hard to develop his oral skills from a very young age and relied heavily on his ability to read lips, only learning sign language later in life.

From ages two to six, he attended the Montgomery County Public School System's Auditory Service program before being enrolled in standard area schools all the way up to his graduation from John F. Kennedy High School.

And it was while at that high school that his gifts became impossible to ignore. During his time there, he became the first basketball player in school history to score more than a thousand points, batted 509, hit five home runs in sixteen games for the baseball team, and was named a Parade Magazine High School All-American in soccer.

He was flying, and the sport that he actually showed the most promise in was soccer; playing as a deadly striker, he stood tall among the rest at FIFA's first Under-16 World Cup in China at a time when Americans rarely did so in the sport.

It was that rarity, the simple fact that soccer didn't provide the same opportunities as other sports in the States, that led Curtis to look elsewhere. Choosing to focus on both basketball and baseball, he would have pursued football, too, if his dad had let him!

Curtis lived and breathed sport; his disability was no match for his athletic ability, although it did provide extra hurdles for him to jump, with soccer opponents trying to rip his hearing aid from his ear and him being unable to hear the referee's whistle. Curtis kept his head down and controlled his own actions, ignoring those of others.

After high school, Curtis was not only drafted by the New York Mets but was also offered a basketball scholarship by the College of William and Mary. Where some may have seen those two opposing opportunities as the time to make a decision—Curtis said yes to both! Playing college basketball at the same time as starting his baseball career with the Mets—*at the same time!*

Once again, Curtis was successful, earning his degree from William and Mary, and after drafting in the minors for seven years, his Major League debut with the Montreal Expos—incidentally, in doing so, he became the first deaf player in the Major League since 1945.

His first MLB hit was a double, and he was given a standing ovation from the crowd that lasted several minutes! *"The crowd was on their feet giving me a standing ovation that lasted for about five minutes," [...] "I felt the cheer. It was so loud, as if the crowd was trying to get me to hear their applause. It was very emotional."*

Although he was never a full-time player in the majors, Pride played 13 seasons and reached his peak in 1996 with the Detroit Tigers—in 301 plate appearances; he hit 300 with a slugging percentage of 513. He also reached career highs of 17 doubles, 5 triples, and 10 home runs!

Curtis made it to the Majors thanks to a combination of hard work, grit, and the absolute focus that his superpower provided him.

After baseball, Curtis focused on giving back—working with *Together With Pride,* an organization that helps children that are hearing impaired. Curtis is also a proud member of the President's Council on Fitness, Sports, and Nutrition and has also worked as a coach at Gallaudet University, which is a college for the hearing impaired—managing to improve the team!

Finally, the MLB named Curtis as their *Ambassador For Inclusion* in 2015.

Curtis may not have had the hall-of-fame careers that others had in this book, but he was still an inspiration to millions for the way that he turned his disability into an *added ability* and squeezed every drop of his ability into multiple sports.

Greatest Sporting Achievement

Being named one of 1985's top 15 soccer prospects in the world—you'll notice that Curtis Pride is the only one whose achievement is for a sport he didn't play professionally in!

PETE GRAY

If they insulted me, I didn't pay attention. I mostly kept to myself.
—Pete Gray

Completing an incredibly brave trio of players with disabilities, Pete was an amputee baseball player who once was told, *"Son, I've got men with two arms who can't play this game"* by a baseball coach when requesting a tryout.

Pete Gray, born Peter Wyshner (he changed his name when he was a teenager to avoid ethnic prejudice), was born in Pennsylvania and had four siblings. His father had previously emigrated from Lithuania, meaning Pete grew up in the baseball-obsessed US—and quickly became just as obsessed as everyone else.

But life threw Pete a curveball.

When he was just six years old, he fell from a wagon, resulting in him trapping his right arm and needing it amputated. His father was tough on him to ensure he didn't feel sorry for himself, tough love that would eventually pay off.

Pete adapted, learning to swing left-handed by hitting rocks with a stick until he was able to handle a thirty-eight-ounce bat. He even invented his own way of catching and throwing, using his chest to help him catch before putting his glove under the stub of his right arm and squeezing on it until the ball rolled from under his stub, across his chest, and into his left hand—incredible!

Pete's determination meant that he would become good enough to play for a semi-professional team, but even that was after bribing the coach with ten dollars!

"Keep it if I don't make good," Pete told Max Rosner, the owner and the manager of the Brooklyn Bushwicks. He did though—hitting a home run in his very first game in front of ten thousand fans, batting .350 across two seasons and earning a minor-league spot with Quebec-based team Trois-Rivieres—where he would hit .381.

Pete was on the rise, playing for the Chickasaws in Memphis, where in 1944, he was named the *Southern Association's Most Valuable Player.* His time in the spotlight arrived when the St. Louis Browns acquired his contract for $20,000, a record at the time for a player from the Southern League.

But unlike the majority of players in this book, Pete's time in the spotlight was brief. Back in 1945, in the midst of World War II, the majors had lost 500 ballplayers to the service, and major league baseball teams were struggling to fill out their roster (the leagues were still segregated at the time—no groundbreaking Jackie Robinson appearance yet).

Despite coming under scrutiny from some of his teammates and being accused of being somewhat of a *freak show performer,* Pete performed well, keeping to himself and winning people over with his work ethic. And it was undeniable that he was helping the team! With him on the field, their winning percentage was .600 and dropped to .425 when he was on the bench—he was there on merit.

But Pete had something else on his mind. Rather than being satisfied with his new role as a major league baseball player, he was desperate to fight for his country. *"Boys, I can't fight, so there is no courage about me,"* Gray explained to the sportswriters that named him *Most Courageous Athlete.*

He was guilty that his disability, despite not stopping him from playing baseball, was stopping him from fighting for his country. *"If I could teach myself how to play baseball with one arm, I sure as hell could handle a rifle."*

But Pete would soon find that he could contribute to the war in his own unique way. He was setting an example at a time when it was needed most. Visiting wounded and disabled soldiers in army hospitals to assure them that they could follow his example and live a productive life. Pete was an absolute inspiration to the entire nation.

Even though Pete didn't enjoy the sporting exploits of others in this book, he was undoubtedly inspirational and managed to transcend sport at a time when his country needed hope.

Greatest Sporting Achievement

Pete Gray played in the Yankee Stadium in front of over 38,000 fans that included his proud parents. Pete stepped up to the plate in the seventh inning to loud *We want Gray* chants!

Chapter 4

SOCCER

S occer, or football, is the world's most popular sport, played in every country and fast-growing in the United States as it tries to catch the coattails of the likes of football, basketball, and baseball...

It is also home to some of the world's most recognizable superstars.

LIONEL MESSI

I prefer to win titles with the team ahead of individual awards or scoring more goals than anyone else. I'm more worried about being a good person than being the best football player in the world. When all this is over, what are you left with? When I retire, I hope I am remembered for being a decent guy.

—Lionel Messi

Lionel Messi is living proof that the heart and spirit can provide strength when the body can't. Although his name needs no introduction, his story is one that everybody should hear.

That isn't because his story was one full of struggle. However, he *did* have his own struggles, but they were far from as desperate as some of the other athletes in this book. Lionel's story is one of humility and staying grounded.

Lionel was born into a poor family, his mom was a part-time cleaner, and his father worked in a steel factory. His talent was obvious early on, and he was outperforming all opponents and outshining all of his teammates. However, when he was aged 11, a hormone deficiency was revealed, which threatened to stunt his growth.

His talent had already caught the eye of Barcelona, who took a chance on him and paid for his treatment, without which he may have had a very different story—his first contract was actually written on a napkin!

Despite Lionel's clear talent, he never shied from hard work, prepared to work harder than all around him, despite his gifts, and motivated by the poor finances of his family. "*You have to fight to reach your dream. You have to sacrifice and work hard for it. I start early and I stay late, day after day, year after year. It took me 17 years and 114 days to become an overnight success."*

But it is *who* Lionel has become that we can truly learn from. Having won, quite literally, everything in the sport, he has remained humble throughout, never letting even the craziest success go to his head.

He has even made it clear that he's uncomfortable with the idea of being a role model and believes that working hard for the team is far more important than any individual awards. Now, is it fair to say that if Lionel Messi, arguably the greatest to ever play soccer, can stay humble, you can stop showing off your new sneakers?

Remember, guys and gals, hard work beats talent when talent doesn't work hard!

Greatest Sporting Achievement

Lionel Messi led his beloved country to win the 2022 FIFA World Cup.

NEYMAR

I do not play football to win the Ballon d'Or. I play football to be happy, because I love it and want to play football. — **Neymar**

When his mother was pregnant with him, Neymar's parents couldn't afford an ultrasound, meaning even they didn't see his talent coming!

Thankfully, he was healthy. But born into humble beginnings, living in a small suburb of Sao Paulo, his parents couldn't afford electricity, and his father had just given up on having a football career of his own.

But in the dark, Neymar would find light, enjoying the candlelight and even having fun. In *Neymar: My Story—Conversations with My Father,* Neymar's father explains, *"What we had in that house with no electricity was priceless: true love. That's how you really build a home, a life. With love. Even without money, our family was united and happy."*

His love of football was also evident early. In fact, he would sleep with over 50 footballs in his bedroom! Neymar would sharpen his skills on the uneven streets of Sao Paulo, as well as playing indoor futsal. The combination of the uneven street needing greater ball control and the demanding, tight nature of futsal was forcing Neymar to build on the incredible talent he had already been blessed with.

However, even as Neymar started to show promise, his father couldn't come and watch him play as he struggled to hold down three jobs. However, his struggle was in vain when Neymar and his family had to move in with his grandparents, sharing a single room and mattress in a desperate attempt to save money.

The lack of money, and the struggle that Neymar endured, helped shape and humble him. When asked in a 2006 interview what he would do if he made lots of money through football, his immediate answer was to help his family. His family may have lacked money and even time for each other, but they never lacked the most precious currency of all—love.

But way back before that interview, Brazilian clubs, as well as some of Europe's giants, were circling Neymar, specifically Real Madrid, who would offer Neymar's father a life-changing offer for his son. Remember, this is the man that had worked three jobs and had moved his family into his grandparents' home to share a mattress.

Recognizing that Neymar wasn't ready, he rejected the offer so that he could stay where he was comfortable, playing for Santos, a professional team in Brazil. He turned down the money because he could see that Neymar was homesick and had stopped enjoying his football. All Neymar Sr. ever wanted was for his son to find joy and love in the game.

The money didn't matter to him, and any money that Neymar *did* get while playing for Santos was earned. His father was strict with his monthly allowance and gave him rewards—such as a car—for good performance.

Neymar's humble beginnings and upbringing would lead to him becoming one of the world's best, a household name, and rich beyond the dreams of any child playing football on the uneven streets of Brazil.

His story is one of humility, hard work, and, most importantly, love. He and his father always put his love of his family and then of the sport that he loved first, even with riches on offer.

But what can we take from this?

Do what you love. If you find your passion and work hard enough to improve at it, maybe success will come, but if it doesn't, your passion will bring you something far more important than money—Love.

Greatest Sporting Achievement

Neymar won the Champions League with Barcelona in 2015.

VICTOR MOSES

When I started going to school, I started getting used to things, like the language. After that, I started adapting to school, friends, and everything. It was really difficult to start with, but I survived. **—Victor Moses**

Victor Moses is the survivor of an upbringing laced with heartache and tragedy, yet always intertwined with soccer.

When Victor was just 11, while out playing soccer barefoot in the streets of Kaduna, the Nigerian city he and his family called home, he was pulled aside and given the devastating news of his parents' deaths.

His father was a Christian pastor, and his mother worked for the church, meaning that when violence erupted between Christians and Muslims, they were right in the line of fire. Before we go any further, I'm sure you are thinking about how sad it is that a difference in belief can cause such violence—and you're exactly right.

Little did Victor know that he was also in danger, so much so that a friend helped hide him for a week before his family scraped together enough money to send him to a foster family in South London, England. Imagine if you got a call this second to tell you that you were moving home to another country that you can't speak the language of—I can't imagine many things scarier than that!

Victor had lost his parents, was trying to process his grief, and was on what must have felt like an alien planet. The one consistent that he still had to provide him comfort was a soccer ball at his feet.

He played out in the South London streets day and night, eventually noticed by a local youth team when he was 13. Victor was so entertaining and exciting on the pitch that he actually started to draw a crowd of hundreds who wanted to see what all the fuss was about.

The local youth team reached out to a professional soccer scout, providing a break that life surely owed him, and he shone, scoring five goals in one game! But that wasn't all; the professional club that signed him to a schoolboy contract also placed him in a private school.

His soccer skills, having already provided him comfort after a tragedy, had now provided him the platform to process it so that he could move forwards.

He has gone on to win six major trophies in his career, including the English Premier League and the one closest to his heart—The African Cup of Nations.

Victor survived and thrived, despite the awful situations that life threw at him. He showed perseverance and bravery in the most frightening of circumstances and never forgot to focus on his goal, knowing that it was the best chance he had at a better life.

We all have days or weeks that throw us curve balls. There are things that happen that are out of control that make us feel helpless. But we never are—you are never helpless. Keep your composure and re-think, change direction, and take one small step towards where you would like to be.

If you have lost a loved one, try to remember that they would want you to continue to grow and live your life. I'll leave you with one more quote from Victor Moses that I think it's important to remember. *"They should be proud of me, looking down being proud."*

Greatest Sporting Achievement

Victor Moses won the English Premier League with Chelsea in 2017.

LUKA MODRIC

The war made me stronger; it was a very hard time for me and my family. I don't want to drag that with me forever, but I don't want to forget about it, either. —**Luka Modric**

Luka Modric is a diamond sifted from the rubble of his war-torn homeland.

But his story is one filled with heartbreak and war, one that many wouldn't have made it through. But Luka did, despite some coaches and then journalists, feeling he was too small to make it as a soccer player. He made it.

Once, a child running through rubble for the safety of an underground shelter with his family, he's now one of the most decorated players in world soccer.

To go back to the start of Luka's story, we start with his grandfather, the man that Luka was named after. Luka's grandfather was a rugged street mender that kept 150 goats and sheep—he was a tough guy, but with Luka, his first grandchild, he melted.

Rather than go to nursery, Luka stayed with his grandparents, learning how to hunt rabbits and herd sheep from a tender age, all under the loving gaze of his grandfather. Luka grew into the role of his grandfather's assistant—buying building materials, repairing things, stacking hay, and shoveling snow. He was teaching him how to be a man.

The closeness of their relationship, however, would only make the tragedy that was to come more painful. At the time, the relations between the Croatians and the Serbians were strained, and Luka's grandfather's reluctance to move away when the Serbians moved in on their mountains would ultimately lead to his being killed.

Luka was too young to fully understand, but years later, when he was 10, he wrote about what had happened while in school: *"The event and the feeling of fear I will never forget took place four years ago when the Chetniks killed my grandfather. I loved him so much. Everyone cried, and I just couldn't understand that my dear grandpa was no more. I used to ask if those who did this, and who made us run away from our home, can even be called people?"*

Luka didn't let such tragedy stop him though, in fact, it was that very steel that was welded to his soul through war and pain that pushed him to live his dream, *"All the things that happened in my childhood helped me to become more tough, to believe in myself and to fight for my dreams."*

Now as an adult, one of the most impressive things about him away from the soccer field is the way that he has completely let go of his anger and pain, holding no ill feelings toward Serbia or its people. Bad things happen, and life goes on.

In football, Luka has gone on to win some of soccer's highest honors, like the Champions League and the Ballon d'Or, rising from the rubble and heartache to make his grandfather proud.

There is much we can learn from Luka's story, like strength, underdog spirit, and letting go of anger. But I'll let the great man tell you for himself:

I say that to young kids: never stop believing in yourself, not even when people tell you that you cannot do this or this. It is the only way you can succeed in something, not just in sport, but in general. You have to believe in yourself, taking motivation from things people are saying. That helped me never to give up. I am a fighter in general and it never crossed my mind to give up because someone said something. **—Luka Modric**

Greatest Sporting Achievement

Luka Modric won the Ballon d'Or in 2018, the highest individual honor available in men's football.

ALIREZA BEIRANVAND

I got up one night and went to Tehran without my parents' permission. I said to myself even if the whole world disagreed, I'd pursue my dreams.
—**Alireza Beiranvand**

Our last soccer player is Alireza Beiranvand, the current goalkeeper of the Iranian National team. His story is a tale of struggle, stones, and sheep!

Alireza was born into a family of sheep-herding travelers in West Iran. He was the oldest of five siblings, which meant that he had the most responsibility, and he became a shepherd very young to help his family out.

His family traveled constantly because they needed fresh grass for their sheep, meaning it was hard for Alireza or his siblings to settle down, not that he had much time for friends, anyway! Working alongside his dad day and night, Alireza didn't realize it then, but he was learning the power of hard work and also working on his reflexes while trying to catch the slippery buggers, which would only help him later.

For Alireza, though, working as a shepherd just wasn't enough. He had a burning desire to play football, having started playing when he was just three years old. When his family finally settled in the village of Sarabias, he started to get a little breathing room from all that wool and spent his spare time playing with friends in the street.

They would play football (surprise, surprise) and a game called Dal Paran, a game that actually involved throwing stones long distances, although back then he had no idea he would be doing the same thing with a soccer ball at the World Cup!

It was also around this time that he started to train with a local side. Like most kids (including some of you probably), he wanted the glory of playing as a striker. But life works in funny ways, and when the team's goalkeepers hurt themselves, Alireza took his place in the net, trading scoring goals for making saves—and he was good!

Despite his clear talent as a shot-stopper, his own father was dead against his dream. *"My father was against me playing football. Not just football, but all sports, and even studying; he said neither would be useful to us as a large family. He tore up my football kit and told me to go to work."*

Despite having to play with his bare hands after his dad tore his gloves, Alireza still refused to give up on his dream. He ignored his dad (something you should only do with caution, by the way!) and saved enough money to buy a ticket to Tehran, the nation's capital, hoping he would find more football teams there.

But at this point, Alireza learned a very important lesson about hard work and luck; luck often finds you when you work hard. Alireza was struggling for money and sleeping on the street. When he met a football coach on the bus one day—a random meeting? Or is the universe trying to help Alireza out?

He didn't have the money to train with the coach's football team, but he persisted, and eventually, the coach saw how desperately he wanted to play football and gave him a chance. And Alireza took that chance with both hands, literally.

He would sleep right outside the doors of the club stadium, working all hours at a dressmaking factory, washing plates, greasing pizza ovens, washing cars, and sweeping streets. He did anything and everything he could to keep his dream alive.

But while playing for Naft Tehran, fate would take another turn. At the time, Alireza was struggling to stay fit while working as a street cleaner, so he started training with another team to solve that problem but was injured while doing so and then was let go by Naft Tehran. When the team he had been training with refused to give him a contract, Alireza was left without a club, and his dream was slipping away.

It was only a call from the Naft under-23 coach that gave him hope, and without that call, he may never have made it as a footballer. He was invited to play for the under-23 and shone—a call-up to play for the National team's under-23 team quickly followed, and he then became Naft's first-team goalkeeper. His refusal to quit and willingness to stick it out when it would have been easier to return home had paid off.

It was while playing for Naft that, in 2014 Alireza caught the eye of the world with his record-breaking assist, throwing the ball over 70 meters to assist his teammate! The throw would eventually be confirmed as a Guinness World Record—all that time playing Dal Paran in the street paid off!

He has gone on to win multiple trophies in Iran, play for club teams around the world, and represent his country Iran over 50 times, including playing in three World Cups! He has also won personal honors too, including being named the Iranian *Footballer of the Year* in 2019!

Alireza is a great example of not giving up and working your hardest to take every opportunity that comes your way. The next time you are feeling like a task is too difficult, try to imagine Alireza chasing sheep around!

Greatest Sporting Achievement

Alireza Beiranvand won the Iranian Player of the Year in 2019.

Chapter 5

INSPIRATIONAL WOMEN

Women in sports are on the rise and are an interesting area of focus due to the discrimination that they have to face, including not being taken as seriously or not being paid as much as their male counterparts.

This rise has given little girls of all backgrounds the belief to chase their own dreams in a world that was once closed off. No child should have to limit their aspirations regardless of gender, and now, thanks to these incredible women, they don't.

JESSICA LONG

From a very early age, I just decided that I was going to be unstoppable and I wasn't going to let my legs hold me back.
—**Jessica Long**

Jessica Long is a paralympic swimmer and sixteen-time gold medalist with another six silvers, four bronzes, and countless World Championship medals, she is now one of the most successful athletes in history and the second most decorated Paralympian in the country's history.

But her journey to success was a long one.

Jessica was born in Siberia when her mother was just 16 years old. But that was far from the toughest part of her journey because she was also born with fibular hemimelia, meaning she was missing the fibula in both her legs, and as a result, they were underdeveloped.

Jessica was adopted by an American family when she was 13 months old who wanted to provide her with better opportunities. Five months later, her legs were operated on and amputated below the knees.

Jessica grew up angry and disappointed, yet determined, enduring so many medical procedures that she got to know the doctors and became far more comfortable on an operating table than any three-year-old should be.

She couldn't understand why she was different, which led to her resenting God, blaming Him for her disability and all of the subsequent surgeries she had to endure, and ignoring her parents' promises that *God had a plan.* All Jessica wanted was to be *normal,* but she wasn't normal—she was special.

She became interested in the physicality of sports and was drawn to gymnastics, but fearing it might cause more damage to her legs when she was 10 years old, she chose to focus on swimming instead.

She was the only girl on the swimming team without legs, but was welcomed and never picked on or made to feel out of place, she never looked back, and there was no doubting her swimming ability when she entered trials to compete for Team USA and qualified for the 2004 Paralympics at 12 years old—just two years after joining the team!

As if that wasn't impressive enough, there's more. She won gold! After two years on the swimming team, she qualifies for Team USA and won gold at her first Paralympics—crazy! It was also while living at the US Olympic and Paralympic Center that she was invited to a Bible study and had a change of heart, giving her life to Christ.

It was shortly after becoming a Christian that Long met her birth mother and was finally able to let go of the anger and resentment she was holding due to her adoption. *"I truly believe that with God's timing, it came at a time where I had just been forgiven of all my sins. How could I not forgive her?"*

She was healing and was fully focused on her sporting accomplishments, the best of which were yet to come.

In 2006, Jessica gave an incredible eighteen record-breaking performances! She won nine gold medals, held five world records, and became the first Paralympic athlete to be awarded the AAU's James E. Sullivan Award.

Now, Jessica's goal is to encourage younger para-athletes to chase their dreams. *"It is absolutely possible: dream really, really big,"* she said. *"There are so many amazing Paralympic athletes out there who are breaking barriers. There are so many possibilities out there, so find your passion, but also know that you are going to have to be consistent and work really, really hard. You define your own success.*

Greatest Sporting Achievement

In 2006, Jessica Long was bestowed the honor of being named the *U.S. Olympic Committee's Paralympian of the Year.*

BETHANY HAMILTON

Courage doesn't mean you don't get afraid. Courage means you don't let fear stop you. **—Bethany Hamilton**

When Bethany Hamilton was just 13, she survived a shark attack, although that left her lucky to be alive, caused her to lose two-thirds of the blood from her body and her left arm. For many, the attack would provide enough of a mental scar to prevent them from ever swimming in the ocean again, but for Bethany, it was a minor speed bump on her way to an incredible career.

Take a second to think about the fear that would come with surviving such an attack and the mental strength it must have taken for her to get back into the ocean, then when you couple that with the physical challenges of not only learning to live with one arm as a teenager but also learning how to surf without a limb that is crucial in doing so— Bethany showed incredible resilience and bravery.

Her passion for surfing simply outweighed her fear of the attack.

By the time she was 13, she had already been surfing for 10 years and competitively for five. Born in Hawaii and raised in a family of surfers, she received her first sponsorship when she was just nine years old, and as a member of the Hanalei Surf Co. team, Bethany was able to win competitions against more experienced surfers.

In 2003 she won her age group in Hawaii's local motion/Ezekiel surf into summer event as well as the open division, besting more experienced surfers once again. She followed those up by finishing second in the open women's division of the NSSA (National Scholastic Surfing Association) National Championships. Catching waves were in her blood.

On the fateful day of the attack, Bethany was rushed to the emergency room and underwent several operations before stabilizing and being allowed home after a few days. The story drew national attention as it was determined that Bethany had been attacked by a 14-foot tiger shark, but more shocking than the attack was the positive outlook of the victim.

Bethany showed incredible resilience and maturity despite the horrific attack and permanent change to her body, vowing to get right back on the board as soon as she could.

Which she did after just a single month.

Bethany initially used a longer and slightly thicker custom surfboard with a handle for her right arm to make it easier to paddle. She also became more reliant on kicking to make up for the loss of her arm. It took Bethany just 26 days. 20—6—To learn how to surf with one arm.

Just two short months after that, she returned to joining competitions—winning the NSSA National competition in Australia! More success would soon follow when she won the same competition the following year and went on to have a stellar career that resulted in seven competition wins and numerous podium finishes.

Bethany is now involved with a number of charities and even has her own foundation called *Friends of Bethany*, which reaches out to young amputees and offers them hope through religion.

The foundation offers retreats for young women who have suffered traumatic limb loss, where they would host free community nights to inspire the sharing of comeback stories. They would host an annual event with guest speakers for girls twelve and up to help empower them. They also have a retreat for young male amputees focused on faith and fitness.

When looking at Bethany's story, it's easy to take inspiration from her courage, work ethic, and perseverance, but we can also learn from her willingness to forgive. She never blamed the creature that would forever change her life and even described sharks as "beautiful creatures" in a 2011 interview with WhatCulture.

Greatest Sporting Achievement

Jessica Long was named the *Best Comeback Athlete* by ESPY in 2004.

KATHRINE SWITZER

All you need is the courage to believe in yourself and put one foot in front of the other. —**Kathrine Switzer**

Kathrine Switzer was born in Amberg before moving to and growing up in Fairfax County, Virginia. As a child, she would play a variety of sports, but more importantly, she was a keen runner, finding empowerment from running a mile each day. Back then, she ran for herself, blissfully unaware that she would eventually run for women everywhere.

After graduating from George Marshall High School, Kathrine attended Lynchburg College, where she competed in the few running events that were available to women at the time.

She then transferred to Syracuse University to study journalism and English literature. It was while at Syracuse that, alongside earning her bachelor's degree, Kathrine would be granted permission to train with the men's cross-country running program.

Taking on longer distances to test herself and meeting Arnie Briggs, a coach who encouraged her to train, but in a brutal example of the way the world was back then, told her that a marathon was a step too far for a *fragile woman* although he did concede that if any woman could, she could—and she did.

After proving to Arnie that she could handle the distance in training, he agreed to take her to Boston to compete in her first marathon.

At that time, there weren't technically any rules against a woman running a marathon, but it was widely known that they couldn't. So Katherine signed up for the race using only her initials, determined to run as an official competitor, cleverly slipped under the radar, and was an official entrant!

Come race day, Kathrine wore a hood to hide her hair and was greeted by other runners with support and enthusiasm, but the good feeling didn't last when a race manager noticed she was a woman when her hood slipped off and tried to rip her number from her sweatshirt. Yes, it really did make him *that* mad that a woman was running!

Kathrine avoided her attacker, thanks to the help of both Arnie and her boyfriend, and completed the race—making history and inspiring women around the world who had been told they were *too fragile.*

Although it would still be another five years before the Boston Marathon would accept female runners, the stand against gender inequality that Kathrine took that day encouraged major change.

Her career continued. In 1974, she was the women's winner of the New York City marathon, and just a year later, she, rather poetically, posted a personal best of 2:51:37 back in Boston.

Runner's World Magazine named Kathrine the *Female Runner of the Decade* from 1967 to 1977, and was inducted into the National Women's Hall of Fame in 2011 for her empowerment of women—Something that she's still doing through her global non-profit, *261 Fearless*—261 is the number she once clutched for dear life when it was nearly ripped from her; now, it represents a collective that uses running to empower and encourage women.

In 2017, Kathrine returned to the Boston Marathon, her ninth appearance in it, on the 50th anniversary of her first. With 261 on her chest once more, this time, she led a team of *261 Fearless* runners through a race populated by a nearly half-and-half split of men and women—how times have changed! The number 261 was subsequently retired in Kathrine's honor, and just a year later, she was awarded an honorary doctorate of humane letters degree.

Kathrine Switzer's legacy is unparalleled, and her impact is still felt to this day.

Greatest Sporting Achievement

Though not a personal achievement as such, Kathrine Switzer founded the Avon International Running Circuit, a series of worldwide races for women that encouraged the inclusion of women's marathon running as an Olympic event.

SERENA WILLIAMS

Luck has nothing to do with it, because I have spent many, many hours, countless hours, on the court working for my one moment in time, not knowing when it would come. —
Serena Williams

Serena Williams is one of the best tennis players to walk the planet of any genre or era, and she has the accolades to back it up. But before she was a tennis powerhouse, she was a little girl from Michigan being pushed to her absolute limit by her father.

When Serena was just three years old, her family moved to California, and her journey to tennis immortality would begin on the pothole-littered courts of Compton. The courts were undesirable, and the streets that surrounded them even less so, but that was all part of Serena's father's plan to warn her of what life had to offer if she didn't work hard.

She was pushed hard, and her father was determined to give her and Venus, her sister, the best chance of success. They left every ounce of energy they had on the court from a tender age and trained relentlessly.

Her father was working hard too, by the way! This isn't the story of two girls that were born into a tennis dynasty but the story of a father that used books and videos to teach himself how to teach them.

As we now know, all that hard work (including daily two-hour practice sessions) and encouragement quite literally paid off, but back then, the girls were faced with hostility and discrimination that only made them more determined to succeed.

At nine years old, Serena's father moved their family again, this time to Florida so his daughters could attend a tennis academy, sensing they needed a higher level of education, and they were even home-schooled so that they could give maximum focus on tennis.

However, when Serena was 10, their father withdrew them from junior tennis tournaments, wanting them to slow down to prevent burnout as well as allowing them to give renewed focus to their school work, perhaps pulling back a little. It was also around this time that racism became a factor. Serena's father had heard some of the white parents being derogatory to his girls.

Serena was impressive, holding a record of 46-3 on the US Tennis Association juniors and ranked number one in her Floridian age group. Serena faced more controversy when she fought to be allowed to turn professional at just 14! She threatened to sue the WTA (World Tennis Association) but dropped it at her parents' behest—she was a fighter, alright!

What followed was a meteoric rise as both Williams sisters shook the foundations of the tennis world. They were much more powerful than women who had come before them, and unashamedly vibrant in their fashion sense despite the plain white attire often associated with tennis.

They were proud of their heritage, often taking to the court with vibrant braids and speaking of empowering young girls of color. Already credited with inspiring African-American children from low-income areas, the Williams sisters have also contributed immensely to those from underprivileged backgrounds. The incredible work of *The Serena Williams Foundation* could quite literally fill a book of its own, but a couple of highlights are the building of a school in Kenya and providing scholarships for underprivileged kids.

> *It all starts with Venus and Serena. The demonstration effect. The power of seeing two African-American girls with braids in the finals of the biggest tournaments in the world in a predominantly white sport. Just a huge impact that really can't be overstated. That attracted thousands of girls into the sport, not just African-American but all backgrounds and races.* **—Martin Blackman, General Manager of Player Development**

Greatest Sporting Achievement

Serena Williams won a total of 23 Grand Slam singles titles, the most of any player, male or female, in the Open Era.

LINDSEY VONN

Setbacks motivate me. —**Lindsey Vonn**

Lindsey Vonn was an alpine skier who simply refused to let her body quit on her.

During her time, Lindsey won everything that alpine skiing had to offer, but in doing so, she pushed her body to its limits, bringing multiple, potentially career-ending injuries, but Lindsey wasn't ready to end her career, so there was no way the injuries were going to, she recovered every time and was never deterred from the sport that she loved.

Born in Minnesota, Lindsey took skis at just two years old, started racing when she was seven, and made history as the first American woman to win Italy's Trofeo Topolino at just 14!

Her father, being a skier with great potential to have won a National Title at 18 before his career was ended by a knee injury, pushed her hard to achieve the things that he couldn't.

Lindsey was improving daily and gaining national attention, being named as a member of Team USA for the Olympics in 2002, while just seventeen. After a solid showing at the Olympics, the next year she won her first silver medal at the Junior World Championship with a handful of medals and podium finishes in the years that followed.

But in 2006 she would be dealt her first major blow, forcing her to dig deep and find the resolve that she would become known for.

Going into the Olympic games, she had high hopes, clocking the second-fastest time in her first practice run. But a crash during the practice run ended up seeing her evacuated by helicopter and hospitalized.

Incredibly, Lindsey returned to the slope two days later and finished eighth. The guts she showed saw her awarded the U.S. Olympic Spirit Award—voted for by fans, fellow athletes, and the media.

It was a comeback that optimizes the athlete that Lindsey would become. Just a year later, she won silver medals in the downhill and super-G at the World Championships, but a crash in training would end her season four weeks early, and the ACL sprain that her knee suffered would cause her problems moving forwards.

Lindsey dominated for the next few years, racking up three consecutive World Cup Championships, a variety of medals, and her fourth overall championship. Little did she know her biggest challenge was yet to come.

She suffered a horrific crash during the 2013 World Championships, tearing both her ACL and MCL as well as fracturing her lateral tibial plateau (the upper part of her shin—ouch!). Her knee needed reconstruction, and she had a long period of rehab ahead.

What Lindsey achieved after those injuries was nothing short of extraordinary. Suffering from injuries that would have ended the careers of many, she endured grueling rehab and fought her way back, through multiple setbacks with her weakened knee to eventually return at the 2018 Olympics, performing admirably against opponents much younger than her to claim a bronze medal, after which she said: *"I won the bronze medal but I feel like I've won the gold medal."*

She would retire the next year after another heavy fall, recognizing her body was growing tired and wanting to preserve her future health. But she went out on her terms, retiring after sharing the podium with players considered to be the future of the sport she loved the year prior.

Lindsey was an absolute warrior, fighting back to fitness time and time again when others would have given up.

Greatest Sporting Achievement

Lindsey Vonn won a bronze medal at the 2018 Olympics.

CONCLUSION

The athletes in this book all have varied upbringings and backgrounds, different genes and different beliefs, and were born with different advantages or disadvantages. But what they all have in common is perseverance. They all endured their respective challenges and kept the belief that they could achieve their dreams.

Find your passion and give it your all! You don't have to win a World Cup or be named an NBA MVP, but your life will be all the richer for recognizing what it is you truly love doing, I assure you.

REFERENCES

Abbott, Jim / Encyclopedia.com. (n.d.). Www.encyclopedia.com. https://www.encyclopedia.com/sports/encyclopedias-almanacs-transcripts-and-maps/abbott-jim

Abhinandhinee. (2021, October 4). *Babe Ruth / The success story of the greatest baseball player of all time. Failure before Success.* https://failurebeforesuccess.com/babe-ruth-success-story/#:~:text=From%20living%20in%20an%20orphanage

Accomplishments. (n.d.). Bethany Hamilton. https://bethanyhamiltonwebsite.weebly.com/accomplishments.html

Achievements - the official licensing website of Jackie Robinson. (n.d.). Jackie Robinson. https://jackierobinson.com/achievements/

Admin. (n.d.). *Curtis Pride – society for American baseball research.* https://sabr.org/bioproj/person/curtis-pride/

Alireza Beiranvand / Football Wiki / Fandom. (n.d.). Football Wiki. https://football.fandom.com/wiki/Alireza_Beiranvand#:~:text=On%2023%20March%202014%2C%20Beiranvand

Alireza Beiranvand. (2023, March 24). Wikipedia. https://en.wikipedia.org/wiki/Alireza_Beiranvand

All about 261 Fearless the global running network: 261 Fearless. (n.d.). Www.261fearless.org. Retrieved March 31, 2023, from https://www.261fearless.org/about-261

All time leaders / Stats / NBA.com. (n.d.). Www.nba.com. https://www.nba.com/stats/alltime

"Babe" Ruth gets his nickname in Fayetteville. (n.d.). Www.ncdcr.gov. Retrieved March 31, 2023, from https://www.ncdcr.gov/blog/2016/03/07/babe-ruth-

gets-his-nickname-fayetteville#:~:text=On%20March%207%2C%201914%2C%20GeorgeBabe Ruth. (n.d.). The MY HERO Project. https://myhero.com/B_Ruth_dnhs_kt_US_2013_ul#:~:text=Ruth%20saved%20thousands%20by%20giving

Beyond the sport: Social justice champion. (n.d.). Spectrumnews1.com. https://spectrumnews1.com/ca/la-west/beyond-the-sport/2022/02/17/beyond-the-sport--kareem-abdul-jabbar-continues-to-inspire#:~:text=Abdul%2DJabbar%20has%20been%20an

Brandman, M. (n.d.). *Biography: Serena Williams.* National Women's History Museum. https://www.womenshistory.org/education-resources/biographies/serena-williams

Champion Paralympic swimmer Jessica Long shares story of adoption and God's grace. Liberty News. (2022, November 9). Liberty News. https://www.liberty.edu/news/2022/11/09/champion-paralympic-swimmer-jessica-long-shares-story-of-adoption-and-gods-grace/#:~:text=Born%20with%20fibular%20hemimelia%20to

Clark, M. (2011, September 24). *SOUL SURFER Interview With Bethany Hamilton!* WhatCulture.com. http://whatculture.com/film/soul-surfer-interview-with-bethany-hamilton.php

Curtis Pride. (2022, January 10). Wikipedia. https://en.wikipedia.org/wiki/Curtis_Pride

Curtis Pride: the deaf USA soccer prodigy who turned to pro baseball. (2015, May 6). The Guardian. https://www.theguardian.com/football/blog/2015/may/06/curtis-pride-the-deaf-usa-soccer-prodigy-who-turned-to-pro-baseball

Dell Curry stats. (n.d.). Basketball-Reference.com. https://www.basketball-reference.com/players/c/curryde01.html

Desk, L. (2022, June 3). *'I've failed over and over again in my life, that is why I succeed': Michael Jordan.* The Indian Express. https://indianexpress.com/article/lifestyle/life-positive/ive-failed-over-and-over-and-over-again-in-my-life-and-that-is-why-i-succeed-michael-jordan-motivational-video-7839233/#:~:text=%E2%80%9CI

Desk, N. S. (n.d.). The incredible success story of Michael Jordan. Thenewsmen. https://thenewsmen.co.in/high%20flyers/the-incredible-success-story-of-michael-jordan/44895

Editors, H. com. (2019, November 17). *Jackie Robinson.* HISTORY. https://www.history.com/topics/black-history/jackie-robinson#:~:text=Robinson

11 inspiring footballers who braved all struggles. (2018, July 4). Pop Culture, Entertainment, Humor, Travel & More. https://www.scrolldroll.com/inspiring-footballers-who-braved-all-struggles/

11 stories from Neymar's childhood that will make you appreciate how hard he's had it. (2016, March 2). Dream Team FC. https://www.dreamteamfc.com/c/archives/uncategorized/162952/11-stories-from-neymars-childhood-that-will-make-you-appreciate-how-hard-hes-had-it/

Elman, J. (2020, August 14). *Jimmy Graham escaped a horrific group home life to become an All-Pro TE.* Sportscasting | Pure Sports. https://www.sportscasting.com/jimmy-graham-escaped-a-horrific-group-home-life-to-become-an-all-pro-te/

Ferrari-King, G. (n.d.). *Most inspiring "From-Rags-to-Riches" sports stories.* Bleacher Report. https://bleacherreport.com/articles/2163388-most-inspiring-from-rags-to-riches-sports-stories

50 inspirational Giannis Antetokounmpo quotes. (2021, April 5). SportyTell. https://sportytell.com/quotes/giannis-antetokounmpo-quotes/

First women graduate from US Army Ranger School as gender barriers continue to fall. ABC News (Australian Broadcasting Corporation). (2015, August 22). Web.archive.org. https://web.archive.org/web/20150822132200/http://www.abc.net.au/news/2015-08-22/women-shine-as-gender-barriers-continue-to-fall-us-army-rangers/6716888

5 Inspiring female athletes and their powerful life stories. (2021, March 21). The Athlete Blog. https://theathleteblog.com/inspiring-female-athletes/

40 Lionel Messi quotes that will inspire you to pursue your dreams. The Highlights App. (n.d.). Www.thehighlightsapp.com. Retrieved March 31, 2023, from https://www.thehighlightsapp.com/blog/lionel-messi-quotes

Giannis Antetokounmpo. (2023, March 30). Wikipedia. https://en.wikipedia.org/wiki/Giannis_Antetokounmpo#:~:text=He%20received%20the%20Most%20Improved

Goldman, J. (2018, April 15). *17 powerful Jackie Robinson quotes on life, success, and equality.* Inc.com; Inc. https://www.inc.com/jeremy-goldman/17-powerful-jackie-robinson-quotes-on-life-success-equality.html

Green, K. (n.d.). *Why Tom Brady is one of the most motivational athletes in the world.* Addicted 2 Success. https://addicted2success.com/motivation/why-tom-brady-is-one-of-the-most-motivational-athletes-in-the-world/

Hardy, B. (2016, April 5). *23 Michael Jordan quotes that will immediately boost your confidence.* Inc.com; Inc. https://www.inc.com/benjamin-p-hardy/23-michael-jordan-quotes-that-will-immediately-boost-your-confidence.html

Hill, G. (2019, October 25). *Bethany Hamilton is "Unstoppable."* CNN. https://edition.cnn.com/2019/10/25/sport/bethany-hamilton-surfing-spt-intl/index.html

Holt, O. (2020, August 15). *Luka Modric reveals the childhood tragedy that shaped his character.* Mail Online. https://www.dailymail.co.uk/sport/football/article-8631277/Luka-Modric-reveals-tragedy-shaped-character-Chetniks-killed-dear-grandpa.html

Executive Speakers Bureau INC. (n.d.). *Jim Abbott.* EXECUTIVE SPEAKERS BUREAU. All Rights Reserved. https://www.executivespeakers.com/speaker/jim-abbott#:~:text=Despite%20being%20born%20with%20only

Hytner, D. (2012, September 14). *Victor Moses: they should be proud of me, looking down being proud.* The Guardian. https://www.theguardian.com/football/2012/sep/14/victor-moses-interview-chelsea

Iyer, R. (2021). *The living legend & Basketball Sensation – Michael Jordan Success Story.* Leader Biography. https://www.leaderbiography.com/michael-jordan-success-story/

Jackie Robinson: The power of self-control in overcoming adversity. (n.d.). Retrieved March 31, 2023, from https://sourcesofinsight.com/jackie-robinson-story-of-self-control/#:~:text=He%20was%20the%20first%20African

Jafarzadeh, B. (2018, June 1). *Alireza Beiranvand: from sleeping rough to the World Cup with Iran*. The Guardian. https://www.theguardian.com/football/2018/jun/01/alireza-beiranvand-sleeping-rough-world-cup-iran-goalkeeper

Jerry Rice. (2021, February 26). Wikipedia. https://en.wikipedia.org/wiki/Jerry_Rice

Jerry Rice biography: NFL football player. (n.d.). Www.ducksters.com. https://www.ducksters.com/sports/jerry_rice.php#:~:text=Jerry%20Rice%20was%20born%20in

Jerry Rice quotes (author of go long!). (n.d.). Www.goodreads.com. Retrieved March 31, 2023, from https://www.goodreads.com/author/quotes/41758.Jerry_Rice#:~:text=%E2%80%9CToday%20I%20will%20do%20what

Jessica Long. (2020, July 13). Wikipedia. https://en.wikipedia.org/wiki/Jessica_Long

Jimmy Graham. (2023a, March 28). Wikipedia. https://en.wikipedia.org/wiki/Jimmy_Graham

Jimmy Graham. (2023b, March 28). Wikipedia. https://en.wikipedia.org/wiki/Jimmy_Graham#Professional_career

Jimmy Graham net worth. (2019, January 25). Celebrity Net Worth. https://www.celebritynetworth.com/richest-athletes/nfl/jimmy-graham-net-worth/

Jimmy Graham quotes. (n.d.). BrainyQuote. Retrieved March 31, 2023, from https://www.brainyquote.com/authors/jimmy-graham-quotes

Kareem Abdul-Jabbar. (2023, January 12). Wikipedia. https://en.wikipedia.org/wiki/Kareem_Abdul-Jabbar#:~:text=At%20the%20time%20of%20his%20retirement%2C%20Abdul%2DJabbar%20held%20the

Kareem Abdul-Jabbar's signature sky hook notably absent in NBA's copycat world. (n.d.). NBA.com. Retrieved March 31, 2023, from https://www.nba.com/news/kareem-abdul-jabbar-skyhook-absent-modern-nba

Kathrine Switzer. (2023, January 27). Wikipedia. https://en.wikipedia.org/wiki/Kathrine_Switzer#Later_competition

Kolberg, B. (2021, October 14). *The humble superstar: New Giannis Antetokounmpo biography explores champion's family life, legacy.* Wisconsin Life. https://wisconsinlife.org/story/giannis-the-improbable-rise-of-an-nba-mvp/

Livacari, G., & Livacari, G. (2016). Babe Ruth and Kids, 1935 | Baseball History Comes Alive! "Baseball History Comes Alive!" https://www.baseballhistorycomesalive.com/babe-ruth-and-kids-1935/#:~:text=Babe%20genuinely%20loved%20kids%20%E2%80%93%20kids

Laible, A. (n.d.). *The inspiring story of Paralympic champion Jessica Long. SI Kids: Sports News for Kids, Kids Games and More.* https://www.sikids.com/kid-reporter/the-inspiring-story-of-paralympic-champion-jessica-long

Lindsey Vonn. (2021, September 13). Wikipedia. https://en.wikipedia.org/wiki/Lindsey_Vonn

Lindsey Vonn - age, injuries & skiing. (2020, December 30). Biography. https://www.biography.com/athletes/lindsey-vonn

Lindsey Vonn quotes. (n.d.). BrainyQuote. Retrieved March 31, 2023, from https://www.brainyquote.com/authors/lindsey-vonn-quotes_2

List of career achievements by Kareem Abdul-Jabbar. (2023, January 2). Wikipedia. https://en.wikipedia.org/wiki/List_of_career_achievements_by_Kareem_Abdul-Jabbar

Luka Modric quotes. (n.d.). BrainyQuote. Retrieved March 31, 2023, from https://www.brainyquote.com/authors/luka-modric-quotes#

Luka Modric - Titles & achievements. (n.d.). Www.transfermarkt.co.uk. Retrieved March 31, 2023, from https://www.transfermarkt.co.uk/luka-modric/erfolge/spieler/27992

Mead, W. (2022, September 9). *Simone Biles - age, brother & gymnastics.* Biography. https://www.biography.com/athletes/simone-biles

Meet swimmer Jessica Long / Disability Today Network. (2013, December 17). Web.archive.org. https://web.archive.org/web/20131217190843/http://www.disabilitytodaynetwork.com/us-paralympics/blog/meet-swimmer-jessica-long

Michael Jordan. (2023, March 29). Wikipedia. https://en.wikipedia.org/wiki/Michael_Jordan#Post-retirement

Michael Jordan biography - life, family, children, story, death, history, wife, school, mother, young. (n.d.). Www.notablebiographies.com. https://www.notablebiographies.com/Jo-Ki/Jordan-Michael.html#:~:text=His%20father%20worked%20as%20a

Michael Oher. (2023, January 25). Wikipedia. https://en.wikipedia.org/wiki/Michael_Oher#Professional_career

Michael Oher news, biography, NFL records, stats & facts. (n.d.). Www.sportskeeda.com. Retrieved March 31, 2023, from https://www.sportskeeda.com/nfl/michael-oher#:~:text=University%20of%20Mississippi-

Motivational story by Jim Abbott on overcoming adversity. (n.d.). Www.aboutonehandtyping.com. http://www.aboutonehandtyping.com/storiesfolder/jimabbottnotgone.html

Motivational Success Story Of Lionel Messi - How The Boy - Lionel Messi. (2020, May 4). Lionel Messi. https://www.lionel-messi.eu/2020/05/04/motivational-success-story-of-lionel-messi-how-the-boy/

Motivelane. (2020, November 28). *Lionel Messi success story / motivating journey.* Motivelane. https://motivelane.com/lionel-messi-success-story-motivating-journey/#:~:text=His%20grandmother%20supported%20Leo%20in

Nefarious. (2021, January 13). *DOUBTED - Stephen Curry (Motivational Mini-Movie)* [Video]. YouTube. https://www.youtube.com/watch?v=Op2m1mSleBs

Newsweek Special Edition. (2016, April 25). *Michael Jordan didn't make Varsity—at first.* Newsweek. https://www.newsweek.com/missing-cut-382954

Neymar - Titles & achievements. (n.d.). Www.transfermarkt.com.

https://www.transfermarkt.com/neymar/erfolge/spieler/68290

Neymar quotes. (n.d.). BrainyQuote. https://www.brainyquote.com/authors/neymar-quotes

Mears, J. (2020b, August 1). "One-armed wonder": 75 years ago, Pete Gray inspired MLB fans. Yardbarker. https://www.yardbarker.com/mlb/articles/one_armed_wonder_75_years_ago_pete_gray_inspired_mlb_fans/s1_13132_32277692

O'Brien, J. (2021, December 4). *Messi discusses importance of staying humble and disliking being a role model.* Mirror. https://www.mirror.co.uk/sport/football/news/lionel-messi-psg-role-model-25618918

106 Kareem Abdul-Jabbar quotes - inspirational quotes at BrainyQuote. (n.d.). BrainyQuote. https://www.brainyquote.com/authors/kareem-abdul-jabbar-quotes

Ott, T. (2021, September 29). *Bethany Hamilton - life, age & family.* Biography. https://www.biography.com/athletes/bethany-hamilton

Pasceri, R. (n.d.). *Deafness didn't hinder Curtis Pride's drive toward a remarkable MLB career.* Bleacher

Report. https://bleacherreport.com/articles/1186245-deafness-didnt-hinder-curtis-prides-drive-toward-a-remarkable-mlb-career

Pete Gray. (2023, February 1). Wikipedia. https://en.wikipedia.org/wiki/Pete_Gray#Major_league_career

Pete Gray overcame a childhood accident to make history. (n.d.). Baseball Hall of Fame. https://baseballhall.org/discover/pete-gray-overcame-accident-to-make-history

Petrova, A. (n.d.). *The 10 most popular sports in the US. The Sporting Blog.* https://thesporting.blog/blog/the-10-most-popular-sports-in-the-us

Seahawks TE Jimmy Graham shares his inspirational story. (2015, May 21). HeraldNet.com. https://www.heraldnet.com/sports/seahawks-te-jimmy-graham-shares-his-inspirational-story/

Serena Williams - husband, daughter & US Open. (2021, April 23). Biography. https://www.biography.com/athletes/serena-williams

Serena William's lasting influence. (n.d.). BBC News. Retrieved March 31, 2023, from https://www.bbc.co.uk/news/av/world-us-canada-34229415

Shahin, A. (2015, January 13). *Neymar - Part 1: From the streets to FC Barcelona.* Barca Blaugranes. https://www.barcablaugranes.com/2015/1/13/7532781/neymar-jr-part-I-skinny-kid-greatness-streets-fc-barcelona

Smith, M. D. (2012, February 2). *Jimmy Graham has let go of the bitterness from his childhood.* ProFootballTalk. https://profootballtalk.nbcsports.com/2012/02/02/jimmy-graham-has-let-go-of-the-bitterness-from-his-childhood/

Sports. (2015, March 27). *Terry Rozier matures after troubled childhood, excels as top scorer for Louisville.* The Daily Orange. https://dailyorange.com/2015/03/terry-rozier-matures-after-troubled-childhood-excels-as-top-scorer-for-louisville/

Sports: Breaking records, breaking barriers / Babe Ruth / Smithsonian's national museum of American history /. (n.d.). Amhistory.si.edu. Retrieved March 31, 2023, from https://amhistory.si.edu/sports/exhibit/superstars/ruth/index.cfm#:~:text=Ruth%20created%20a%20sensation.

Staff, NBA. com. (2021, September 14). *Legends profile: Michael Jordan.* Www.nba.com; NBA. https://www.nba.com/news/history-nba-legend-michael-jordan

Stephen Curry. (n.d.). NBADraft.net. https://www.nbadraft.net/players/stephen-curry/

Stephen Curry. (2021, August 31). Wikipedia. https://en.wikipedia.org/wiki/Stephen_Curry#Awards_and_honors

Stephen Curry, Golden State Warriors / Fellowship of Christian athletes. (2014, January 24). Web.archive.org. https://web.archive.org/web/20140124024839/http://www.fca.org/themagazine/stephen-curry-golden-state-warriors/

Stephen Curry - UNBROKEN - 2021 motivation. (n.d.). Www.youtube.com. Retrieved March 31, 2023, from https://www.youtube.com/watch?v=TUsZWTVlDTM

Super Bowl LVII totals more than 113 million viewers, ranks second most-watched game ever. (n.d.). Nielsen. https://www.nielsen.com/news-center/2023/super-bowl-lvii-totals-more-than-113-million-viewers-ranks-second-most-watched-game-ever/#:~:text=NEW%20YORK%20%E2%80%93%20February%2014%2C%202023

SurferToday.com, E. at. (n.d.). *The inspirational quotes by Bethany Hamilton.* Surfertoday. https://www.surfertoday.com/surfing/the-inspirational-quotes-by-bethany-hamilton#:~:text=Courage%20doesn

Team, T. S. (2021, February 11). *The Tom Brady success story.* The STRIVE. https://thestrive.co/tom-brady-success-story/

Tennis.com. (n.d.). *Serena Williams records that may never be broken: A career golden slam in singles and doubles.* Tennis.com. https://www.tennis.com/news/articles/serena-williams-unbreakable-records-career-golden-slam-singles-doubles

Terry Rozier quotes. (n.d.). BrainyQuote. Retrieved March 31, 2023, from https://www.brainyquote.com/authors/terry-rozier-quotes

Thank you, Kareem Abdul-Jabbar, for always championing social justice. (2023, February 6). ESPN.com. https://www.espn.co.uk/nba/story/_/id/35602384/kareem-abdul-jabbar-life-social-justice-champion-record-no-athlete-break

The Editors of Encyclopedia Britannica. (2019). Serena Williams | Biography, Titles, & Facts. In Encyclopædia Britannica. https://www.britannica.com/biography/Serena-Williams

The real story of Victor Moses and his journey from Kaduna to the world. (2018, September 21). TheCable. https://www.thecable.ng/real-story-victor-moses-journey-kaduna-world

The true story of Michael Oher and "The Blind Side." (2021, February 11). Biography. https://www.biography.com/movies-tv/the-blind-side-true-story-michael-oher

TIME 100: Heroes & icons - Jackie Robinson | page 1. (2000, May 27). Web.archive.org. https://web.archive.org/web/20000527060639/http://www.time.com/time/time100/heroes/profile/robinson01.html

Top 25 quotes by Jim Abbott | A-Z Quotes. (2015). A-Z Quotes. https://www.azquotes.com/author/19880-Jim_Abbott

Top 25 quotes by Kathrine Switzer | A-Z quotes. (2015). A-Z Quotes. https://www.azquotes.com/author/18873-Kathrine_Switzer

25 Babe Ruth quotes - inspirational quotes at BrainyQuote. (n.d.). BrainyQuote. https://www.brainyquote.com/authors/babe-ruth-quotes

Unknown. (n.d.). *Terry Rozier's hard-fought journey to the NBA.* Www.celticslife.com. Retrieved March 31, 2023, from https://www.celticslife.com/2015/10/terry-roziers-hard-fought-journey-to-nba.html

Venus and Serena against the world. (2017, September 3). Web.archive.org. https://web.archive.org/web/20170903121131/http://connection.ebscohost.com/c/articles/1012925/venus-serena-against-world

Victor Moses - from tragedy to trophies. (n.d.). BBC Sport. Retrieved March 31, 2023, from https://www.bbc.co.uk/sport/football/42060348

Victor Moses quotes. (n.d.). BrainyQuote. Retrieved March 31, 2023, from https://www.brainyquote.com/authors/victor-moses-quotes

Victor Moses - Titles & achievements. (n.d.). Www.transfermarkt.co.uk. Retrieved March 31, 2023, from https://www.transfermarkt.co.uk/victor-moses/erfolge/spieler/59866

Voutsela, T. (2022, August 24). *Giannis Antetokounmpo: The origin story of basketball's living Greek legend.* Olympics.com; International Olympic Committee. https://olympics.com/en/news/giannis-antetokounmpo-origin-story-basketball-legend

Walter Payton. (n.d.). *The MY HERO Project.* Retrieved March 31, 2023, from https://myhero.com/walter-payton#:~:text=Walter%20Payton%20inspired%20many%20individuals

Walter Payton, extraordinary running back for Chicago Bears, dies at 45. (1999, November 2). The New York Times. https://www.nytimes.com/1999/11/02/sports/walter-payton-extraordinary-running-back-for-chicago-bears-dies-at-45.html

Why is baseball so popular in the USA – Sports Encyclopaedia. (n.d.).

https://sportsecyclopedia.com/tank/why-is-baseball-so-popular-in-the-usa/#:~:text=It

Wikipedia Contributors. (2018a, November 28). *Babe Ruth.* Wikipedia; Wikimedia Foundation. https://en.wikipedia.org/wiki/Babe_Ruth

Wikipedia Contributors. (2018b, December 19). *Terry Rozier.* Wikipedia; Wikimedia Foundation. https://en.wikipedia.org/wiki/Terry_Rozier

Wikipedia Contributors. (2019a, February 25). *Tom Brady.* Wikipedia; Wikimedia Foundation. https://en.wikipedia.org/wiki/Tom_Brady

Wikipedia Contributors. (2019b, March 11). *Serena Williams.* Wikipedia; Wikimedia Foundation. https://en.wikipedia.org/wiki/Serena_Williams

Wikipedia Contributors. (2019c, March 26). *Bethany Hamilton.* Wikipedia; Wikimedia Foundation. https://en.wikipedia.org/wiki/Bethany_Hamilton

Wikipedia Contributors. (2019d, March 28). *Walter Payton.* Wikipedia; Wikimedia Foundation. https://en.wikipedia.org/wiki/Walter_Payton

Wikipedia Contributors. (2019e, April 21). *Kareem Abdul-Jabbar.* Wikipedia; Wikimedia Foundation. https://en.wikipedia.org/wiki/Kareem_Abdul-Jabbar

Wikipedia Contributors. (2019f, November 16). *Luka Modrić.* Wikipedia; Wikimedia Foundation. https://en.wikipedia.org/wiki/Luka_Modri%C4%87

Wikipedia Contributors. (2020, January 28). *Walter Payton NFL Man of the Year Award.* Wikipedia; Wikimedia Foundation. https://en.wikipedia.org/wiki/Walter_Payton_NFL_Man_of_the_Year_Award

With more black women, U.S. open shows Serena and Venus legacy. (2020). The New York Times. https://www.nytimes.com/2020/09/04/sports/tennis/us-open-black-players-serena-venus-williams.html

Made in the USA
Las Vegas, NV
19 December 2023